# The Intensive Retreat for Couples

# His Workbook

The Intensive Retreat for Couples

His Workbook

By

Onedia N. Gage, Ph. D.

Other Books by
# Minister Onedia N. Gage

Are You Ready for 9<sup>th</sup> Grade . . . Again? A Family's Guide to Success

As We Grow Together Daily Devotional for Expectant Couples

As We Grow Together Prayer Journal for Expectant Couples

The Best 40 Days of Your Life: A Journey of Spiritual Renewal

The Blue Print: Poetry for the Soul

From Two to One: The Notebook for the Christian Couple

Her Story: Bible Study

Her Story: Daily Devotional

Her Story: The Legacy of Her Fight

Her Story: The Legacy Journal

Her Story: Prayers and Journal

ILY! A Mother Daughter Success Kit

In Her Own Words: Notebook for the Christian Woman

In Purple Ink: Poetry for the Spirit

The Intensive Retreat for Couples: Her Workbook

Love Letters to God from a Teenage Girl

The Measure of a Woman: The Details of Her Soul

The Notebook: For Me, About Me, By Me

The Notebook for the Christian Teen

On This Journey Daily Devotional for Young People

On This Journey Prayer Journal for Young People

One Day More Than We Deserve Daily Devotional for the Growing Christian

One Day More Than We Deserve Prayer Journal for the Growing Christian

Promises, Promises: A Christian Novel

Tools for These Times: Timely Sermons for Uncertain Times

With An Anointed Voice: The Power of Prayer

Yielded and Submitted: A Woman's Journey for a Life Dedicated to God

Yielded and Submitted: A Woman's Journey for a Life Dedicated to God Intimate Study

Yielded and Submitted: A Woman's Journey for a Life Dedicated to God Prayers and Journal

# Library of Congress

The Intensive Retreat for Couples

His Workbook

Purple Ink, Inc. Press

For Information address:
Purple Ink, Inc
P O Box 41232
Houston, TX 77241
www.purpleink.net
www.onediagage.com

ISBN:

978-1-939119-51-3

Printed in the United States

# Dedication

for

Couples

Who need direction

Who need prayer

Who need support

Who need hope


I hope to remove divorce as an option.

I pray to inspire the desire to move toward a great solution:

A Better Marriage!

# God's Word

[24] Therefore shall a man leave his father and his mother, and shall cleave unto his wife: and they shall be one flesh.

**Genesis 2:24 (ASV)**

[6] So that they are no more two, but one flesh. What therefore God hath joined together, let not man put asunder.

**Matthew 19:6 (ASV)**

[32] and be ye kind one to another, tenderhearted, forgiving each other, even as God also in Christ forgave you.

**Ephesians 4:32 (ASV)**

# Dear Lord:

I thank You for this opportunity to write this project. I pray that I have pleased You in this work.

I pray that this reaches hundreds of thousands of married couples and that those couples who are not married become closer to You and even marry. I pray that the couples are able to seek You for direction and hear you clearly about the direction You want them to take in their marriage.

Dear Father, thank You for loving us. Thank You for reminding us of Your love and what to do to love others. So often the issues we have stem from not knowing that we are loved.

Lord, remind us why You led us to one another. Our paths only crossed because of Your plans. Help us to see in each other what You see in us. Help us to forgive so that the other person can feel it and know it and embrace it. Lord, remind us that You are the supplier of our love and You equip us to love others.

Dear Lord, help us to have an abundance of love toward my wife!

Lord, I am not always right so please forgive me and my foolishness.

Lord, I praise You and worship You for the gifts and the service for which You equipped us.

Lord, I thank You for relationships. And the ability to work at them to make them relationships which pleases You. In Jesus' name, I pray!

Amen.

# Dear Man:

Marriage is hard! I understand that sentiment, however, it is possible to have a lasting marriage. Keep in mind that the divorce rate is 53%, so that means that 47% made it. How did they do it? I know that very question is one we all have asked.

Man, do you want your marriage? Do you want your relationship? I have been there. I have decided to divorce. Does that make it a great decision? No, not necessarily. What we do know is that we are responsible for what God says for us to do.

Do you want your marriage and your wife? If so, then pursue her and your marriage outrageously and outlandishly.

Men marry for different reasons than women. Remember that when you are listening to her complaints and her requests. What do you challenge yourself on in your marriage? In this marriage, you have to work and work hard, especially when you do not feel like it.

You do the work because you love your wife but you are committed to and in a covenant with God. When you do not give your best to your marriage, you robbed God, rather than your wife.

I pray for your relationships. I pray for your wholeness and a healthy spirit as you work through your relationship and discover yourself within the confines of this marriage.

Man, you need her to respect you but she has no clue how to truly respect you by your definition. That requires your input and work. You as the man need to love her, which is a tall order. This is the key to your marriage, but you have to overcome the STUFF that stops that from happening.

Man, you have the power to be the game changer in your relationship. She is waiting on you to lead her into greatness. She has dreamed about this marriage for years. She waited for this moment for years. She wants it be great. She needs it to be great. And so do you. This relationship is critical to her and rewarding for you.

## The Intensive Retreat for Couples

What does it take to make it great? What does it take to satisfy your need for peace while balancing her need for love and attention?

You may be concerned and consumed but I want you to focus on the following:

1. Pray
2. Repent
3. Confess your feelings
4. Remember why you loved her in the first place
5. Commit to your marriage
6. Recommit to God for your marriage
7. Decide that you are going to be your best self in your marriage
8. Decide that your outcome is going to be pleasing to God!

I am looking forward to great outcomes for your marriage. Share your testimony with me. I can be reached at onediagage@onediagage.com, @onediangage, and on facebook. I want to know the progress you are making.

In God's Service,

Onedia N. Gage

# Table of Contents

# The Covenant

I vow to

- Listen with my heart to my wife, expecting only the best from her without the judgement of the past.
- Forgive her of all the past hurts and the pains which has inhibited our marriage.
- Love extravagantly, with all of my heart and my mind and my soul.
- Pursue her and my marriage outlandishly and outrageously.
- Nurture the health of my relationship through positive talk and thoughts.
- Consider the feelings of my wife.
- Be honest and totally transparent with my wife.
- Be honest and totally transparent with myself.
- Look forward with anticipation the best outcome for my marriage.
- Forgive yourself of all the past hurts and the pains which has inhibited our marriage.
- Remember the great times that we have had and will pursue these times again.
- Believe in my marriage and its strength.
- Believe that my marriage can survive and will be successful.
- Share my victorious testimony about the revival of my marriage.
- Avoid the negative talk about my wife and my marriage.
- Listen to my heart about my needs and desires for myself, my wife, and my marriage.

I enter this covenant with love, truth, and faith.

_____        _____

The Husband                                                           Date

# Instructions for Use

This journal is designed to accompany the in person retreat which I host several times each year. Whether you are in class with me or doing it alone, the results should be an improved relationship based on following the directions.

1. Read each statement and question carefully. A correct and complete understanding will lead to a better comprehension while answering and addressing those areas authentically.
2. Answer with the depths of your soul. DO NOT answer to please someone else or what you believe is more correct than what you truly feel.
3. Stay focused on the immediate topic. Use the note section for tangents.
4. Remember this is not graded, yet a living and breathing document which is simply your heart on paper.
5. DO NOT anticipate what your wife will answer, think or feel. Answer based on what you truly feel. This is an opportunity to express how you feel without the influence of your other.
6. Be willing to see your marriage from a different, fresh, possibly different perspective.
7. Be HONEST! It is time to be honest with everyone. Your marriage depends on it.
8. Hear your wife with an open heart, prepared to forgive and renew yourself and your wife for ALL that has happened in your relationship.
9. Be prayerful. God has the first and last decision in your relationship.
10. Expect the BEST. Remain positive. Remind yourself about the positive aspects of your relationship and wife.
11. Share the positive outcomes to encourage others.

# Introductions

Who you are impacts your relationship. Your moods, your attitudes, your emotions, your happiness, your anger, and all attributes affect your marriage.

Your details matter! Those details drive choices your wife makes—some consciously and some unconsciously.

Below is the "All About Me" Quiz. Please complete it twice—once about her; the other is the answer key for her. Please use the last five spaces to create questions of your own.

Just a note: please share with her when the answers to the items on the quiz change.

# All About Me

1. What are five of my favorite movies?
2. What is my ideal meal?
3. Where is my favorite place to read?
4. What are my favorite titles?
5. Who are my favorite authors?
6. What is my dream vacation?
7. What is my favorite color?
8. What is my favorite time of day
9. What do I do to escape?
10. Where do I go to escape?
11. What is my favorite time of day?
12. What is my favorite time of year/season/month?
13. What do I do to relax?

14. What is my favorite type of music?
15. Who is my favorite musician(s)?
16. What is my favorite dessert?
17. What is my favorite drink?
18. What is my favorite liquor (if I were going to drink)?
19. What is my favorite musical instrument?
20. What are the instruments that I want to learn to play?
21. What makes me cry?
22. What makes me laugh?
23. What do I do for fun?
24. What inspires me?
25. What are 5 things I want to achieve?
26. What is my favorite snack?
27. What is my favorite sport?
28. What is my favorite sport's team?
29. What is my favorite poem?
30. What is my favorite poet?
31. Who do I call when it's going well?
32. Who do I call when it is not going well?
33. Where do I want to travel?
34. What is my favorite flavor of ice cream?
35. What is my favorite brand of ice cream?
36. What do I do for exercise?
37. What is my pet peeve?
38. What is my favorite style of underwear?
39. What is my favorite television show?
40. Why do I like those movies?
41. Why do I like this show?
42. What excites me?
43. What shuts me down?
44. What do I fear?
45. What makes me happy?

46. What makes me smile?
47. Do I prefer sunshine or rain?
48. Where do I seek guidance and information?
49. What do I need?
50. What are my strengths?
51. What are my weaknesses?
52. What is my favorite car?
53. What is my favorite truck/SUV?
54. What is my favorite car color?
55. What is my favorite restaurant?
56. What is my favorite store?
57. What is my favorite pet?
58. What is my ideal profession?
59. What does my mother think I should be?
60. What does it take for my love tank to be full?
61. What do I do when I am sad?
62. What do I do when I am happy?
63. Who would I like to meet and spend time with (public and famous)?
64. How do you know when I am happy?
65. How do I like to be kissed?
66. How do I like to be held?
67. What is my favorite lovemaking position(s)?
68. Why are birthdays so important to me?
69. What do I dream of?
70. What is my definition of success?
71.
72.
73.
74.
75.

# All About Her

1. What are five of my favorite movies?
2. What is my ideal meal?
3. Where is my favorite place to read?
4. What are my favorite titles?
5. Who are my favorite authors?
6. What is my dream vacation?
7. What is my favorite color?
8. What is my favorite time of day
9. What do I do to escape?
10. Where do I go to escape?
11. What is my favorite time of day?
12. What is my favorite time of year?
13. What do I do to relax?
14. What is my favorite type of music?
15. Who is my favorite musician(s)?
16. What is my favorite dessert?
17. What is my favorite drink?
18. What is my favorite liquor (if I were going to drink)?
19. What is my favorite musical instrument?
20. What are the instruments that I want to learn to play?
21. What makes me cry?
22. What makes me laugh?
23. What do I do for fun?
24. What inspires me?
25. What are 5 things I want to achieve?
26. What is my favorite snack?
27. What is my favorite sport?

28. What is my favorite sport's team?
29. What is my favorite poem?
30. What is my favorite poet?
31. Who do I call when it's going well?
32. Who do I call when it is not going well?
33. Where do I want to travel?
34. What is my favorite flavor of ice cream?
35. What is my favorite brand of ice cream?
36. What do I do for exercise?
37. What is my pet peeve?
38. What is my favorite style of underwear?
39. What is my favorite television show?
40. Why do I like those movies?
41. Why do I like this show?
42. What excites me?
43. What shuts me down?
44. What do I fear?
45. What makes me happy?
46. What makes me smile?
47. Do I prefer sunshine or rain?
48. Where do I seek guidance and information?
49. What do I need?
50. What are my strengths?
51. What are my weaknesses?
52. What is my favorite car?
53. What is my favorite truck/SUV?
54. What is my favorite car color?
55. What is my favorite restaurant?
56. What is my favorite store?
57. What is my favorite pet?
58. What is my ideal profession?
59. What does my mother think I should be?

60. What does it take for my love tank to be full?
61. What do I do when I am sad?
62. What do I do when I am happy?
63. Who would I like to meet and spend time with (public and famous)?
64. How do you know when I am happy?
65. How do I like to be kissed?
66. How do I like to be held?
67. What is my favorite lovemaking position(s)?
68. Why are birthdays so important to me?
69. What do I dream of?
70. What is my definition of success?
71.
72.
73.
74.
75.

# Where Are We?

# Why Are We Here?

Where are we?

Why are we here?

These questions cause us to evaluate our relationship. The evaluation will reveal that you and your wife are in two different places. No matter how you assess that information, you will discover that you are either a little different or EXTREMELY different. The issue is NOT the difference, rather that you are newly realizing that there are such differences. The second surprise is how major the differences are.

The unspoken, undefined issues can create a physical and spiritual and intimate distance. This distance is the real problem in your marriage.

When you ask and answer 'where are we,' and that answer is immensely different, I am going to help you to reach a place such that you are not so far away. The ability to agree on a location is key to reaching the goal.

Why are we here? At this place in our relationship? Wishing we were elsewhere? Wondering how this happened? To us? What do we do now? How do we return to a great place?

We only need to confess TRUTHFULLY where we are individually to one another so that we can arrive at the goal place.

After we discover our issues, then we will develop a plan for overcoming those obstacles as well as shortening our distance.

Let us start finding out where we are and why we are here.

Define marriage. Your personal definition, not the dictionary, nor culture or societal.

_____

_____

_____

_____

_____

_____

_____

_____

_____

_____

_____

_____

_____

_____

_____

_____

_____

_____

_____

Where are we?

Why are we here?

Share your view of your marriage in its current state.

_____

_____

_____

_____

_____

_____

_____

_____

_____

_____

_____

_____

_____

_____

_____

_____

Share your desires for your marriage.

What do you want your marriage to be?

_____

_____

_____

_____

_____

_____

_____

_____

_____

_____

_____

_____

_____

_____

_____

_____

What is your marriage missing?

What is the most difficult part of your marriage?

_____

_____

_____

_____

_____

_____

_____

_____

_____

_____

_____

_____

_____

_____

_____

_____

_____

What is great about your marriage?

_____

_____

_____

_____

_____

_____

_____

_____

_____

_____

_____

_____

_____

_____

_____

_____

_____

_____

_____

_____

_____

Why did you choose to engage in this intensive study?

How did you come to agree to this study and retreat?

_____

_____

_____

_____

_____

_____

_____

_____

_____

_____

_____

_____

_____

_____

_____

_____

_____

## The Intensive Retreat for Couples

What actual event caused you to arrive here? What was the 'last straw?'

_____

_____

_____

_____

_____

_____

_____

_____

_____

_____

_____

_____

_____

_____

_____

_____

_____

_____

_____

_____

_____

What happened when you mentioned this retreat to your wife?

Were there conditions or bargains made in order to arrive here at this retreat?

_____

_____

_____

_____

_____

_____

_____

_____

_____

_____

_____

_____

_____

_____

_____

_____

_____

Grade your relationship.

What is the ideal grade your relationship should have?

What was the highest grade your relationship your relationship has ever had?

What does it take to arrive at the ideal place for your marriage?

_____

_____

_____

_____

_____

_____

_____

_____

_____

_____

_____

_____

_____

_____

_____

# The Ideal Marriage

God invented marriage for man and woman so that each person would have some help through God's assignments in your life. God created marriage for the fulfillment of the covenant between a man and a woman. This covenant started with God and still includes God. The Ideal Marriage honors God and holds to His commands, keeps His covenant, facilitates His work and shares His love with each and others.

The ideal marriage encourages and forgives. It studies and seeks God for righteousness and direction. It builds and supports. It is a bridge and a covering. Ideal marriages are happy, healthy, and whole. Ideal marriages love, foster healing, and keep no record of wrongs. The ideal marriage is harmonious and is romantic.

The ideal marriage is made up of two ideal people who are imperfect and flawed but has the BEST intentions for the other person.

The way to have an ideal marriage is to be an ideal person.

Everyone who is married has a definition of an ideal marriage. Have you shared your definition with your spouse through your actions, words and deeds? Through your attitude? Your intentions? The key to the ideal marriage: YOU!

The Ideal Marriage is based on who you are individually. Because of that, we need to investigate our unique definitions of an ideal marriage and how we personally contribute to that definition.

Be sure to understand that it is hard to require someone to do something that you are not willing to do personally. Further, you have greater influence when you demonstrate the expected behavior—consistently.

How do I define The Ideal Marriage?

How will I communicate my definition of my ideal marriage to my wife?

What does it take to reach that definition in my marriage?

_____

_____

_____

_____

_____

_____

_____

_____

_____

_____

_____

_____

_____

_____

_____

What is my daily schedule?

What time belongs to my wife?

_____

_____

_____

_____

_____

_____

_____

_____

_____

_____

_____

_____

_____

_____

_____

_____

_____

_____

_____

What portion of my life does my husband know?

If you died, what would your husband find out about you?

Is there anything that would embarrass your husband?

_____

_____

_____

_____

_____

_____

_____

_____

_____

_____

_____

_____

_____

_____

_____

_____

Are you welcoming with your tone when you speak with your wife?

Are you excited about the communication between you and your wife?

_____

_____

_____

_____

_____

_____

_____

_____

_____

_____

_____

_____

_____

_____

_____

_____

_____

_____

How would you like to achieve the ideal relationship?

What time does that require?

What activities does that entail?

What level of communication is needed for the ideal marriage to be reached?

_____

_____

_____

_____

_____

_____

_____

_____

_____

_____

_____

_____

_____

_____

_____

_____

_____

What motivates you to be the ideal husband?

What can you do to motivate your wife to be a better wife?

_____

_____

_____

_____

_____

_____

_____

_____

_____

_____

_____

_____

_____

_____

_____

_____

_____

_____

_____

_____

What stops your marriage from being ideal?

_____

_____

_____

_____

_____

_____

_____

_____

_____

_____

_____

_____

_____

_____

_____

_____

_____

_____

_____

_____

# Communication

Communication is defined as the imparting or interchange of thoughts, opinions, or information by speech, writing, or signs.

By definition, communication requires action.

Communication means that you are engaged with the other person, actively and consistently. Communication is key to relationships. Your wife needs that communication. Further, your wife or yourself may THRIVE on that communication. Communication is an investment. Communication validates the other person's needs. Communication clears up misunderstandings. Communication is the answer to most issues in your relationship.

How will you communicate? What will you communicate? In what tone will you communicate? In what location will you communicate? Who will hear you communicate?

When I said, "Your communication is my air, by which I live and off of which I thrive." He was speechless. While he never really responded, his behavior demonstrated that he had no clue what I meant, what I needed, nor why I said it.

The level of communication you need to be successful is defined by your wife, not by you. The communication he needs is defined by him. You are designed to meet that need.

Successful communication is built on transparency. Transparency builds trust. Trust makes communication easier. When you trust the words, actions and deeds of the other person, love is easier to do and be. It is easier to love someone who does not lie to you and tells you the whole truth. Those are two different details.

Communication is not blind and is not dumb. Remember that communication is not love, so it keeps score. Communication keeps track and has an outstanding memory of the not so great communication misunderstandings.

Great communication is a decision. It is a choice. It is no accident when you elect not to communicate clearly with your wife. It is not an accident when you elect to lie or hide something from your wife, especially when you are asked directly about the matter.

Do you want to be married or do you want to be private?

Define what you expect of your wife for communication.

What can your wife expect of you?

_____

_____

_____

_____

_____

_____

_____

_____

_____

_____

_____

_____

_____

_____

_____

_____

_____

_____

What do you do to communicate with your wife?

What happens when you do not communicate with your wife?

_____

_____

_____

_____

_____

_____

_____

_____

_____

_____

_____

_____

_____

_____

_____

_____

_____

_____

What happens when your wife does not communicate with you?

What happens when your do not hear from your wife for an extended period of time?

_____

_____

_____

_____

_____

_____

_____

_____

_____

_____

_____

_____

_____

_____

_____

_____

_____

_____

## The Intensive Retreat for Couples

What would happen if you discovered that your wife kept as many secrets as you, told as many lies as you, and withheld as much information as you?

How would you feel?

How would you respond?

_____

_____

_____

_____

_____

_____

_____

_____

_____

_____

_____

_____

_____

_____

_____

_____

_____

_____

What does it take for you to stop the lack of communication?

How could you change in such a manner that your wife would embrace your commitment to communicate?

Has your wife given up on your ability to communicate with her?

_____

_____

_____

_____

_____

_____

_____

_____

_____

_____

_____

_____

_____

_____

_____

_____

_____

# Can You Hear Me?

## Active Listening

Listening and hearing have been proven different. However, we treat them the same. Verizon made the question: "Can you hear me now?" famous a few years ago. It is a source of hurt in most relationships and has been this way for years.

Listening is an active practice designed to hear and understand what your wife has said. Gage defines the difference as listening incites action. Action should result from listening. Hearing is a passive behavior, which does not require anything. Hearing may not even require a conversation.

Listening is a verb, requiring action; expecting results. Active listening involves asking questions and gaining clarity. Active listening warrants follow through and more dialogue.

Listening involves intimacy and attention to detail. Listening and acting on what you are listening to should bring you closer.

Technically, listening and hearing are synonymous. Often used interchangeably as needed, however, in order to close the gap between you and your wife, action is required. If nothing ever happens after a conversation, you are not listening. Note for the speaker: please understand that effective listening requires effective delivery.

This means that you cannot leave ANY conversation saying or believing that 'he knows what I mean' or 'he knows what I meant.' If you did not SAY it out loud, then words were not heard! Your wife cannot take action on something you never said. If you are not willing to share, then you DO NOT want the action you thought about.

Effective conversation, also known as communication, is only achieved when you are able to say what you are feeling or thinking or dreaming of.

It is imperative we do not claim effective communication when we blame him for ineffective listening.

The listener should not need an interpreter to know what the talker means. That can be annoying, particularly when the listener is held accountable for what you meant but never said.

This is critical when you are trying to eliminate the space between the two of you.

Can you hear me now is only a valid question if you are sharing effectively.

Last thing on this serious topic which is the source of most of your fights: live by the same rules which you expect others to live by. You cannot request transparent, honest communication, active listening, and action-based responses when you lie, share half the story and do nothing about the needs or interests of your wife.

Do you feel that your wife hears and responds to you as you need?

If not, why not?

If yes, is it consistent?

_____

_____

_____

_____

_____

_____

_____

_____

_____

_____

_____

_____

_____

_____

_____

_____

_____

_____

_____

_____

What does it mean to you when your wife hears you?

_____

_____

_____

_____

_____

_____

_____

_____

_____

_____

_____

_____

_____

_____

_____

_____

_____

_____

What do you want to your husband to do to show you that she heard you?

How do you feel when your husband does not hear or does not take action on what she heard?

_____

_____

_____

_____

_____

_____

_____

_____

_____

_____

_____

_____

_____

_____

_____

_____

_____

Do you withhold valuable information which could equip your wife to be better?

If so, why?

_____

_____

_____

_____

_____

_____

_____

_____

_____

_____

_____

_____

_____

_____

_____

_____

_____

_____

_____

_____

How could you make your wife feel more valuable?

_____

_____

_____

_____

_____

_____

_____

_____

_____

_____

_____

_____

_____

_____

_____

_____

_____

_____

What are you thinking about when your wife is talking?

What are you doing when your wife is talking?

Are you hoping she would just shut up?

Are you just waiting on your ability to respond without really listening to what your husband actually said?

_____

_____

_____

_____

_____

_____

_____

_____

_____

_____

_____

_____

_____

_____

_____

What would make you engage your wife better?

_____

_____

_____

_____

_____

_____

_____

_____

_____

_____

_____

_____

_____

_____

_____

_____

_____

_____

_____

_____

# Trust

As we enter into the subject of trust, I am hoping that you decide to do whatever it takes for your wife to trust you.

Trust as a noun is the reliance on the integrity, strength, ability, surety of that person or thing; confidence. Trust is related to security, certainty, belief, assurance, and faith. "Trust implies instructive unquestioning belief in and reliance upon something."

Trust is valuable and is foundational in any relationship. There are elements which build trust and there are other elements which erode that trust. Our job in our relationships is to guard the trust your wife has for you. Likewise, do our best to not erode the trust that you have with your wife.

The trust, once eroded or lost, is hard to regain; not impossible, but really hard.

Trust is maintained similar to way it is earned. Be clear in your communication. Be transparent in your dealings. Be open to your wife when he questions or when he asks you. Tell the truth and this avails you to certain consequences. Make decisions based on how your husband will respond if she knows or will find out.

Your wife's security is based on what you do and do not do. It is your job to offer her the ability to trust you. It is your responsibility to insure that she trusts you. Trust can be achieved after it is lost based on your attitude about the activity which led to the distrust.

You may be thinking how can that be? Well here are some suggestions:

1. Share the passwords to all of your accounts.
2. Delete all contact information of past relationships.
3. Do not open new email addresses at work or otherwise which you do not plan to use to email your wife.
4. Do not open a separate credit cards or bank accounts without the knowledge of your wife.

5. Do not connect socially on social media even if it is for business purposes if you are attracted to the person in any manner.
6. Share times when you are tempted by another man, either visually or mentally, or otherwise.
7. Be honest about your thoughts, needs or desires.
8. Do not become defensive about any questions your wife asks you about your whereabouts, behavior, and activities.
9. Remember that trust is mutual. Protect it with your communication and connections.
10. Ask for forgiveness. Keep asking until you are forgiven. Do not become defensive not quit while you are waiting to be restored.

Trust should be like the oxygen to a relationship. Without trust, the relationship will have a hard time sustaining.

Trusting.

Trusted.

Trust.

Define trust and your trust philosophy.

_____

_____

_____

_____

_____

_____

_____

_____

_____

_____

_____

_____

_____

_____

_____

_____

_____

_____

_____

How valuable is trust to you between you and your wife?

Does your wife trust you?

Do you trust your wife?

_____

_____

_____

_____

_____

_____

_____

_____

_____

_____

_____

_____

_____

_____

_____

_____

_____

_____

What do you do to earn the trust of your wife?

_____

_____

_____

_____

_____

_____

_____

_____

_____

_____

_____

_____

_____

_____

_____

_____

_____

_____

What do you to maintain the trust of your wife?

_____

_____

_____

_____

_____

_____

_____

_____

_____

_____

_____

_____

_____

_____

_____

_____

_____

_____

What do you to erode the trust of your wife?

Why do you continue to erode that trust?

_____

_____

_____

_____

_____

_____

_____

_____

_____

_____

_____

_____

_____

_____

_____

_____

_____

_____

Is it important for your wife to trust you?

Why or why not?

_____

_____

_____

_____

_____

_____

_____

_____

_____

_____

_____

_____

_____

_____

_____

_____

_____

_____

_____

If your trust was breached, what does it take to earn it back?

If I were the one who has to be forgiven, what would you do because of what you did?

_____

_____

_____

_____

_____

_____

_____

_____

_____

_____

_____

_____

_____

_____

_____

_____

_____

_____

_____

What does trust and communication have in common?

How did you reach that philosophy?

_____

_____

_____

_____

_____

_____

_____

_____

_____

_____

_____

_____

_____

_____

_____

_____

_____

_____

_____

Does your husband cause you to not trust her?

What happens/happened?

_____

_____

_____

_____

_____

_____

_____

_____

_____

_____

_____

_____

_____

_____

_____

_____

_____

_____

## The Intensive Retreat for Couples

Can you put your phone facing up and share your lock pattern and voicemail passwords?

Can your wife do it as well?

_____

_____

_____

_____

_____

_____

_____

_____

_____

_____

_____

_____

_____

_____

_____

_____

_____

_____

_____

Can you share all of your social media user names and passwords with your wife?

Can your wife share them with you?

_____

_____

_____

_____

_____

_____

_____

_____

_____

_____

_____

_____

_____

_____

_____

_____

_____

_____

What would happen if you picked up the wrong phone when you left for work?

Will you still be married when you get home?

_____

_____

_____

_____

_____

_____

_____

_____

_____

_____

_____

_____

_____

_____

_____

_____

_____

_____

_____

Are you worthy of your wife's trust?

Would you trust you?

_____

_____

_____

_____

_____

_____

_____

_____

_____

_____

_____

_____

_____

_____

_____

_____

_____

When are you concerned about your wife's behavior and activities, what do you do?

_____

_____

_____

_____

_____

_____

_____

_____

_____

_____

_____

_____

_____

_____

_____

_____

_____

_____

_____

_____

Are you transparent with your wife?

Do you make your wife beg and probe for information?

_____

_____

_____

_____

_____

_____

_____

_____

_____

_____

_____

_____

_____

_____

_____

_____

_____

_____

_____

Are you completely honest with your wife?

Why not?

What does it take to be honest with your wife?

_____

_____

_____

_____

_____

_____

_____

_____

_____

_____

_____

_____

_____

_____

_____

_____

Are you causing your wife to question or second guess your honesty?

Why?

What can you do to stop his fears?

_____

_____

_____

_____

_____

_____

_____

_____

_____

_____

_____

_____

_____

_____

_____

_____

## The Intensive Retreat for Couples

Are you able to do everything on the suggestion list about regaining or/and maintaining your wife's trust?

_____

_____

_____

_____

_____

_____

_____

_____

_____

_____

_____

_____

_____

_____

_____

_____

_____

_____

_____

_____

_____

If you trust is eroded, how long can your relationship continue to exist?

_____

_____

_____

_____

_____

_____

_____

_____

_____

_____

_____

_____

_____

_____

_____

_____

_____

_____

## The Intensive Retreat for Couples

Write a letter to your wife. Either thank her or apologize for the level of the trust in your relationship.

_____

_____

_____

_____

_____

_____

_____

_____

_____

_____

_____

_____

_____

_____

_____

_____

_____

_____

_____

_____

_____

# Love

Love is one of my favorite words. It is quite the emotion. Love is an action!

With such a great word and powerful interaction, why are so many people having trouble in the love category? Based on the divorce rate and the number of marriages licenses issued daily, we have an indication that love is active. The question is though, is it active in your heart? Is love active for your marriage and your relationship?

Consider a few details. Love is only active in your relationship, if you and your wife both say so. Love is necessary for the survival of your relationship. Love is where you started.

With these facts in mind, do you believe that your relationship needs some of your undivided attention?

Your wife needs love! She thrives on your love. When she does not FEEL that love her, even if she can personally prove otherwise, she is not functional and will not be her best. Your wife breathes because of your love. There are no suitable substitutes. No amount of food, shopping, or exercise will do for her what your love does for her.

Love is powerful. Love overrides the foolishness and misunderstandings and lies and even embarrassment.

Love is essential for woman. When she feels and knows your love, you as the husband will reap rich rewards, including her respect and affection.

Love is not to be toyed with or played with. Likewise, love is not a tool to use to get your way or hold things over the head of your wife's life. Your wife wants you to love her and she wants to love you with all of her heart.

Please understand how powerful love is in your marriage and your relationships.

Love is powerful. Love covers a multitude of sins (1 Peter 4:8).

**The Intensive Retreat for Couples**

Love keeps a woman interested in respecting a man. Love keeps a woman eager to please her husband. Love keeps that same woman forgiving her husband. Love covers the issues and helps those issues remain small and inconsequential. Love keeps that woman engaged and involved in your relationship. Love facilitates peace and wards off anger. Love is worth offering and maintaining; growing and growing; responding to and sharing with.

Love her beyond your means!

Define love.

Do you and your wife agree on the definition?

_____

_____

_____

_____

_____

_____

_____

_____

_____

_____

_____

_____

_____

_____

_____

_____

_____

_____

Do you love your wife?

Why?

_____

_____

_____

_____

_____

_____

_____

_____

_____

_____

_____

_____

_____

_____

_____

_____

_____

_____

Does your wife love you?

How do you know?

_____

_____

_____

_____

_____

_____

_____

_____

_____

_____

_____

_____

_____

_____

_____

_____

What is your love language? (www.**5lovelanguages**.com/profile)

Were you surprised about this love language?

_____

_____

_____

_____

_____

_____

_____

_____

_____

_____

_____

_____

_____

_____

_____

_____

_____

_____

Are you hard to love?

Why or why not?

_____

_____

_____

_____

_____

_____

_____

_____

_____

_____

_____

_____

_____

_____

_____

_____

_____

_____

_____

Is your wife hard to love?

Why or why not?

Is it easy for you to love your wife?

_____

_____

_____

_____

_____

_____

_____

_____

_____

_____

_____

_____

_____

_____

_____

_____

_____

Are you in love with your wife?

Is your wife in love with you?

How do you know?

_____

_____

_____

_____

_____

_____

_____

_____

_____

_____

_____

_____

_____

_____

_____

_____

_____

_____

How does authentic love affect your relationship?

How does it help with responses and behavior?

_____

_____

_____

_____

_____

_____

_____

_____

_____

_____

_____

_____

_____

_____

_____

_____

_____

_____

_____

_____

Do others see the love you share with your wife?

_____

_____

_____

_____

_____

_____

_____

_____

_____

_____

_____

_____

_____

_____

_____

_____

_____

_____

What makes your love special between you and your wife?

_____

_____

_____

_____

_____

_____

_____

_____

_____

_____

_____

_____

_____

_____

_____

_____

_____

_____

What is significant about your love?

_____

_____

_____

_____

_____

_____

_____

_____

_____

_____

_____

_____

_____

_____

_____

_____

_____

_____

_____

_____

How do you explain and describe the love you have for your wife?

_____

_____

_____

_____

_____

_____

_____

_____

_____

_____

_____

_____

_____

_____

_____

_____

_____

_____

_____

_____

How would you explain the following verse: "Love covers a multitude of sins?"

_____

_____

_____

_____

_____

_____

_____

_____

_____

_____

_____

_____

_____

_____

_____

_____

_____

_____

How do you keep the love alive and fresh in your relationship?

_____

_____

_____

_____

_____

_____

_____

_____

_____

_____

_____

_____

_____

_____

_____

_____

_____

_____

_____

_____

What do you when the love seems weaker or faint?

_____

_____

_____

_____

_____

_____

_____

_____

_____

_____

_____

_____

_____

_____

_____

_____

_____

_____

**The Intensive Retreat for Couples**

Describe some 'just because' love moments or behaviors.

_____

_____

_____

_____

_____

_____

_____

_____

_____

_____

_____

_____

_____

_____

_____

_____

_____

_____

_____

Describe how you demonstrate love for your wife.

_____

_____

_____

_____

_____

_____

_____

_____

_____

_____

_____

_____

_____

_____

_____

_____

_____

_____

What can you do to show your wife more love?

_____

_____

_____

_____

_____

_____

_____

_____

_____

_____

_____

_____

_____

_____

_____

_____

_____

_____

_____

_____

_____

What can your wife do to show you more love?

_____

_____

_____

_____

_____

_____

_____

_____

_____

_____

_____

_____

_____

_____

_____

_____

_____

_____

_____

Does your wife tell you that she loves you enough?

_____

_____

_____

_____

_____

_____

_____

_____

_____

_____

_____

_____

_____

_____

_____

_____

_____

_____

_____

Do you share your loving feelings with your wife enough for her?

_____
_____
_____
_____
_____
_____
_____
_____
_____
_____
_____
_____
_____
_____
_____
_____
_____
_____

How do your childhood relationship experiences with your parents affect your relationship?

_____

_____

_____

_____

_____

_____

_____

_____

_____

_____

_____

_____

_____

_____

_____

_____

_____

_____

_____

_____

_____

What does love make you do differently?

_____

_____

_____

_____

_____

_____

_____

_____

_____

_____

_____

_____

_____

_____

_____

_____

_____

**The Intensive Retreat for Couples**

Write your wife a love letter.

_____

_____

_____

_____

_____

_____

_____

_____

_____

_____

_____

_____

_____

_____

_____

_____

_____

_____

_____

_____

# Respect

You thrive on respect. It is your oxygen. Respect reminds you that you are the man—the husband—HER husband. You need it but she will not give it to you. You do not understand why she will not. You deserve it. You do everything that you should to earn her respect. Besides even if you did not deserve the respect, you should still be respected. That is what most men think; that is where the trouble starts.

Respect: earned or given? Age old discussion and debate. Whatever your position in the matter, you have to WORK to maintain RESPECT. The difference between what she things and what you think is huge. You believe that respect is yours—always. She feels that you have to keep working to be respected. She may lose respect for you because of your words or your deeds or your attitude.

A woman respects a man who:

- Keeps his word
- Is honest
- Is loving
- Is responsible
- Is kind
- Is insightful
- Is a communicator
- Is a listener
- Is active in your marriage
- Is worthy of her respect

Respect is not dependent on being loving to her but it really helps.

What does respect mean to you? Does she know what that looks like? Do you share what is disrespectful to you? Did you share what is disrespectful to you? Did she seem surprised by your interpretation of what is disrespectful? It would be advisable, just like you discussed finances that you discuss what this means to you. You need to EXPLICITLY explain your definition of respect, disrespect and share when the definition changes. She deserves a detailed explanation. Like a grocery list! Especially if she asks, which may be in word or deed. This REQUIRES your attention!

How can you share this information? Specifically. Lovingly. Caringly. Timely. Adoringly. Creatively. There are also times she may need a subtle reminder about respect.

Last thing, be sure to remember that when she needs a lesson in respect, check on how she feels about love. If she is not feeling loved, it will be harder for her to be respectful.

The time you spend educating her on respect and appreciating her when she does is time well spent.

How do I show her respect as well:

1. Come home at a respectable time. In most cities, malls, restaurants, and other venues are closing at 9 pm. Go home.
2. Do not come into the house talking on the telephone.
3. Give/offer her your undivided attention.
4. Let her finish her sentences and thoughts.
5. Listen to understand rather than finding fault. Present a solution to what you consider an as issue.
6. Figure out what is important to her. Ask enough questions to understand what makes her tick. Interesting facts. What does she share with her friends? What keeps her wake while you are sleeping?
7. Understand her interests. Hobbies. Her work. Her addictions. Her fears. Her favorites. Use this information to relate to her.
8. Take inventory of her family life; her background is essential to understanding her definition of respect.
9. Find out who she respects and why she respects him or her so that you can how she measures that respect.
10. Keep her first right after God. Remind her that no matter what you have or achieve or know, she is still most important.
11. Remind yourself why you fell in love and why you are in each other's lives in the first place.

It is amazing how she will respond and RESPECT you when you renew your interest in her. Remember that she has a mind, heart and personality just as you do. She is influenced by the world just as you, however your behavior can draw her to you or your behavior can cause her disrespect. Use your relationship and the power of your influence to compel her toward you. Use your best self to draw her to you and she will respect you because of who you are and how you behave.

Define respect.

How will you share your definition with your wife?

_____

_____

_____

_____

_____

_____

_____

_____

_____

_____

_____

_____

_____

_____

_____

_____

_____

Does your wife respect you?

Consistently? If not, when does she disrespect you?

In what manner, does she disrespect you?

_____

_____

_____

_____

_____

_____

_____

_____

_____

_____

_____

_____

_____

_____

_____

_____

_____

Is her disrespect proactive (she does it on purpose or without knowledge of her disrespect) or reactive (based on what you do)?

_____

_____

_____

_____

_____

_____

_____

_____

_____

_____

_____

_____

_____

_____

_____

_____

_____

_____

_____

Have you discussed her respect and disrespect with her?

Does she understand your perspective?

Did you listen to her response?

What did you offer to her as insight?

_____

_____

_____

_____

_____

_____

_____

_____

_____

_____

_____

_____

_____

_____

_____

_____

How do you plan on helping her to respect you?

What are you going to do?

_____

_____

_____

_____

_____

_____

_____

_____

_____

_____

_____

_____

_____

_____

_____

_____

_____

_____

_____

When she disrespects you, what is your response?

What do you say? How do you approach her?

_____

_____

_____

_____

_____

_____

_____

_____

_____

_____

_____

_____

_____

_____

_____

_____

_____

_____

_____

How long after the disrespectful situation do you share about the incident?

What is her response? How does her response make you feel?

Were you surprised by her reaction?

_____

_____

_____

_____

_____

_____

_____

_____

_____

_____

_____

_____

_____

_____

_____

_____

_____

_____

What is the consequence for her disrespect (i.e. moody, non-communicative, etc.)?

Is that an appropriate response?

Does it yield the results that you really desire or does it have the opposite effect?

_____

_____

_____

_____

_____

_____

_____

_____

_____

_____

_____

_____

_____

_____

_____

_____

Is respect given or earned?

Does that fit how you feel about those who respect or disrespect you?

_____

_____

_____

_____

_____

_____

_____

_____

_____

_____

_____

_____

_____

_____

_____

_____

_____

_____

Because respect is so important, do you think it deserves more of your education and attention toward your wife?

Based on this information, how will you share respect with your daughter? Son?

_____

_____

_____

_____

_____

_____

_____

_____

_____

_____

_____

_____

_____

_____

_____

_____

_____

_____

Respond to the following statement: "Her respect is my oxygen."

How can you make this work in your marriage?

_____

_____

_____

_____

_____

_____

_____

_____

_____

_____

_____

_____

_____

_____

_____

_____

_____

_____

Does your pride prevent you from sharing respect with your wife?

What does it take to place your pride to the side in order to reach the understanding of respect?

_____

_____

_____

_____

_____

_____

_____

_____

_____

_____

_____

_____

_____

_____

_____

_____

# Divorce Explored

Divorce should not be an option. It is beyond the last resort! Divorce is permanent solution to often temporary situations. Divorce leaves scars. Divorce should be viewed as a non-option!

The ripple effect of divorce is huge—bigger than you may ever realize. Divorces are becoming more frequent—almost popular. The problem is divorce does not end your relationship. Remember if you have children, you will need to communicate with that spouse because of the children.

Before you reach for divorce as a solution, interview some people who are divorced, and at least one woman. Keep in mind that divorce is not the only solution; often, it is not the best solution.

Divorces happen because pride is overwhelming. Someone needs to say 'I do not want this to end' and 'what does it take to make this work?' Someone needs to listen to his heart and someone needs to realize that this may be solvable if and only if you are willing to do some work—some major, some minor.

Visit the family who have endured divorce and ask yourself which life you would prefer. Can your situation be overcome? Can your situation be solved with some different activities?

Is your situation bad enough to end this and possibly start over with someone else? Consider carefully the use of that option. The feelings which are hurt are going to be your children.

Can this be fixed? If no, then divorce. Be ready for the ugly. If yes, then put all else aside and authentically and genuinely work on your relationship and improve the health of your marriage.

Lastly, stop using divorce as a threat to influence change in your marriage.

Can you live without your wife?

Are you going to regret the decision of divorce?

_____

_____

_____

_____

_____

_____

_____

_____

_____

_____

_____

_____

_____

_____

_____

_____

_____

_____

_____

Can your issues be solved?

How are you making that determination?

What 'extra' does it take to solve them?

_____

_____

_____

_____

_____

_____

_____

_____

_____

_____

_____

_____

_____

_____

_____

_____

_____

Will you be able to parent amicably?

How are you going to feel/react about someone having influence in raising your children, especially when it challenges the agreement you and your wife made previously?

_____

_____

_____

_____

_____

_____

_____

_____

_____

_____

_____

_____

_____

_____

_____

_____

_____

_____

Can you see your wife with someone else without wanting your wife or becoming sick about your situation?

_____

_____

_____

_____

_____

_____

_____

_____

_____

_____

_____

_____

_____

_____

_____

_____

_____

_____

Will you use the court system to make your wife 'pay' for what he has done or not done in your marriage?

_____

_____

_____

_____

_____

_____

_____

_____

_____

_____

_____

_____

_____

_____

_____

_____

_____

_____

_____

_____

Can you walk away with no regrets or without questions?

_____

_____

_____

_____

_____

_____

_____

_____

_____

_____

_____

_____

_____

_____

_____

_____

_____

_____

_____

_____

**The Intensive Retreat for Couples**

Document your family history: previous divorces, never marrieds and the length of existing marriages, along with a health grade of each marriage.

Will your divorce challenge your families?

_____

_____

_____

_____

_____

_____

_____

_____

_____

_____

_____

_____

_____

_____

_____

_____

_____

_____

How are your children going to feel?

How will this impact your friends? Church friends? Social circles?

_____

_____

_____

_____

_____

_____

_____

_____

_____

_____

_____

_____

_____

_____

_____

_____

_____

_____

Is your situation life threatening?

Are your circumstances as bad as they can get?

_____

_____

_____

_____

_____

_____

_____

_____

_____

_____

_____

_____

_____

_____

_____

_____

_____

_____

_____

# Fighting Fair

Conflict is defined as a fight, battle, or struggle, especially a prolonged struggle; strife, as a noun. Conflict is going to happen; you will not agree on all things at all times. However, the use of conflict as a noun rather than a verb is the start of some relational success.

Do not purpose to FIGHT. There will be disagreements but resolve can be present as well.

All fights should be FAIR. If there has to be a fight, then decide. DECIDE to fight fairly. Often I find that when we are hurt, hurting, and maybe even angry, we fight like we do not love and much less like our wife that we are fighting.

Rules of Fighting Fair:

1. Decide that there is a resolve that can be reached.
2. Decide to reach a resolve with a win-win attitude.
3. Do not design a solution where your wife loses.
4. Stick to the matter at hand. Do not add to the issue and do not bring up unrelated, old issues.
5. Control your attitude. Remain calm while speaking and listening.
6. Pray before, during and after your discussion.
7. Be honest with your facts, feelings, and opinions about the matter.
8. Listen to your wife!
9. Remember you love this woman. Your wife loves you and you love her. Treat your wife like you love her.
10. Focus on what God would want you to do.
11. How can we reach a resolve and each party can feel edified?
12. As you work on the solution, remember this relationship is for a lifetime; this situation is temporary.
13. Research the best solution.
14. Uncover how this developed initially, so that we can prevent this from happening again.

15. Write down your resolution so that you can keep your word.

When you solve conflict responsibly, you will feel better. You will be more comfortable in your relationship when neither party has lost or leaves the conflict hurting or broken. Great conflict resolution leads to great communication and a greater relationship.

Do you pick fights?

Do you start most of the fights?

_____

_____

_____

_____

_____

_____

_____

_____

_____

_____

_____

_____

_____

_____

_____

_____

_____

_____

Do you try to avoid fights?

How do you try to avoid fighting?

_____

_____

_____

_____

_____

_____

_____

_____

_____

_____

_____

_____

_____

_____

_____

_____

_____

_____

_____

What are most of your fights about?

_____

_____

_____

_____

_____

_____

_____

_____

_____

_____

_____

_____

_____

_____

_____

_____

_____

_____

_____

_____

How long do your fights last?

How have your fights ended?

_____

_____

_____

_____

_____

_____

_____

_____

_____

_____

_____

_____

_____

_____

_____

_____

_____

_____

Do you feel differently about your wife after a fight?

Does that feeling depend on the outcome of the fight?

_____

_____

_____

_____

_____

_____

_____

_____

_____

_____

_____

_____

_____

_____

_____

_____

_____

_____

_____

Who is the reconciler in the relationship?

Are you a peacemaker?

Do you have the ability to be a peacemaker?

What does it take to be a peacemaker?

_____

_____

_____

_____

_____

_____

_____

_____

_____

_____

_____

_____

_____

_____

_____

Have you ever studied conflict resolution?

Are you using any of the principles you learned in the class?

_____

_____

_____

_____

_____

_____

_____

_____

_____

_____

_____

_____

_____

_____

_____

_____

_____

_____

How do you seek to understand your wife?

How do you seek to be understood?

How would you like to be understood?

_____

_____

_____

_____

_____

_____

_____

_____

_____

_____

_____

_____

_____

_____

_____

_____

_____

_____

Can you fight and still love your wife?

_____
_____
_____
_____
_____
_____
_____
_____
_____
_____
_____
_____
_____
_____
_____
_____
_____
_____
_____
_____
_____

Is it a challenge to respect your wife after a fight?

_____

_____

_____

_____

_____

_____

_____

_____

_____

_____

_____

_____

_____

_____

_____

_____

_____

_____

_____

_____

Do you apologize when you are wrong or at fault?

Is it easy?

Why or why not?

_____

_____

_____

_____

_____

_____

_____

_____

_____

_____

_____

_____

_____

_____

_____

_____

Do you consider yourself easy to get along with?

Why or why not?

_____

_____

_____

_____

_____

_____

_____

_____

_____

_____

_____

_____

_____

_____

_____

_____

_____

_____

_____

_____

Can you forget about the fight once it is resolved?

Why or why not?

_____

_____

_____

_____

_____

_____

_____

_____

_____

_____

_____

_____

_____

_____

_____

_____

_____

_____

_____

How long does it take you to forgive your wife when you have been hurt?

Does your wife have to beg for your forgiveness?

Does your wife have to bargain for your forgiveness?

_____

_____

_____

_____

_____

_____

_____

_____

_____

_____

_____

_____

_____

_____

_____

_____

_____

# Intimacy

Sex! Sex! Sex! You like it. You love it. You want some more of it. You need it. You crave it. You think of it often. Sex. Whew! If only your wife felt the exact same way. But often she does not. She had a headache last month. The month prior, the kids were sick. The month before that, she was tired. You cannot actually remember the last time you were intimate. You are at wits end, no longer knowing what to do. While this may not be your exact story, you have heard it somewhere before. It is not new or totally foreign.

Let's talk about sex versus intimacy. The road to sex reads intimacy! Your wife is a unique creature which needs attentiveness and finesse. Women need to be reminded to why sex is beneficial. You are practical and sex is always a great moment. Women do not see sex the same way. Women consider sex as the bonus of a romantic evening or the result of an insightful conversation or the outcome of hand holding, an extended hug, or some other intimate touching which was carefully yet intentionally and intensively done.

Intimacy needs to be managed carefully, given its required undivided attention, and never neglected. Intimacy should be a comforting place and an exciting place of retreat. Intimacy is a place that we should anticipate enjoying with the person who we love. Likewise, intimacy is not for negotiation. Intimacy is not about making deals and bargaining and bartering. Intimacy involves giving the other person the most vulnerable parts of ourselves. Complete intimacy includes receiving the other person openly, willingly and without prejudice.

Intimacy is a closeness that should not be sacrificed under any conditions. We should protect the intimacy of our relationship. We should value it and remember why we like the intimacy we share.

Your wife's sexual attitude and libido changes based on child birth, age, hormone changes, fatigue, and emotional disconnection based on any number of factors.

There is an easy way to have more sex with your wife: meet her needs. If she says, 'let's talk,' then listen. If she says she needs your time, then give it to her. Meet her needs and she **will** meet yours. After you meet her needs, resolving that need to be heard, then she will do so—most often without you have to say a word.

More importantly, put sex on her mind! I did a radio show a few years ago with this title, where I shared the tools you need for more sex. Compliment her. Solve the need to be heard before 6 PM. Help her with her household/mother duties. Give her some time to herself before 9 PM. Remind her why you love her. Stimulate her brain and her heart.

Then sex is easy.

1 Corinthians 7:2-6 The Message (MSG)

2-6 Certainly—but only within a certain context. It's good for a man to have a wife, and for a woman to have a husband. Sexual drives are strong, but marriage is strong enough to contain them and provide for a balanced and fulfilling sexual life in a world of sexual disorder. The marriage bed must be a place of mutuality—the husband seeking to satisfy his wife, the wife seeking to satisfy her husband. Marriage is not a place to "stand up for your rights." Marriage is a decision to serve the other, whether in bed or out. Abstaining from sex is permissible for a period of time if you both agree to it, and if it's for the purposes of prayer and fasting—but only for such times. Then come back together again. Satan has an ingenious way of tempting us when we least expect it. I'm not, understand, commanding these periods of abstinence—only providing my best counsel if you should choose them.

Are you having enough sex?

Are you having sex often enough?

_____

_____

_____

_____

_____

_____

_____

_____

_____

_____

_____

_____

_____

_____

_____

_____

_____

What is missing from your intimacy?

What needs to improve to satisfy your intimacy needs?

What works for you now?

What do you want more of?

How do you share what you need more of with your wife?

_____

_____

_____

_____

_____

_____

_____

_____

_____

_____

_____

_____

_____

_____

How does your wife define intimacy?

How are your definitions different?

How do you manage those differences?

_____

_____

_____

_____

_____

_____

_____

_____

_____

_____

_____

_____

_____

_____

_____

_____

_____

What are the areas of your relationship which influence your intimacy levels?

Are these areas which you contribute to the strain on your intimacy (i.e. behavior, attitude, etc.)?

_____

_____

_____

_____

_____

_____

_____

_____

_____

_____

_____

_____

_____

_____

_____

_____

_____

_____

_____

_____

What area(s) of your relationship does your husband contribute to the decrease and absence of intimacy?

Have you made her aware of those areas?

Do you have a plan/suggestion for how to overcome these areas or solve this issue?

_____

_____

_____

_____

_____

_____

_____

_____

_____

_____

_____

_____

_____

_____

_____

_____

_____

Have you been completely honest about your intimate needs?

Why not?

When do you plan on being completely honest?

_____

_____

_____

_____

_____

_____

_____

_____

_____

_____

_____

_____

_____

_____

_____

_____

_____

Do you use excuses to avoid sex with your wife (i.e. headache, exhaustion, work, children, etc)?

What does it take to abandon these excuses?

_____

_____

_____

_____

_____

_____

_____

_____

_____

_____

_____

_____

_____

_____

_____

_____

_____

_____

Do you like your wife?

If not, why not?

_____

_____

_____

_____

_____

_____

_____

_____

_____

_____

_____

_____

_____

_____

_____

_____

_____

_____

_____

_____

Is intimacy easy?

If not, why not? If so, why?

_____

_____

_____

_____

_____

_____

_____

_____

_____

_____

_____

_____

_____

_____

_____

_____

_____

_____

Is there one thing that could revive your intimacy?

What is the best part of your intimacy?

What is the worst part of your intimacy?

_____

_____

_____

_____

_____

_____

_____

_____

_____

_____

_____

_____

_____

_____

_____

_____

_____

Has either of you been unfaithful?

_____

_____

_____

_____

_____

_____

_____

_____

_____

_____

_____

_____

_____

_____

_____

_____

_____

_____

Has the trust been otherwise eroded between the two of you?

If so, what happened?

Can it be resolved?

What does it take to regain each other's trust?

_____

_____

_____

_____

_____

_____

_____

_____

_____

_____

_____

_____

_____

_____

_____

_____

_____

_____

Describe your best intimate moment(s).

Real or dreamed.

_____

_____

_____

_____

_____

_____

_____

_____

_____

_____

_____

_____

_____

_____

_____

_____

_____

_____

_____

_____

What can you do to create an environment where intimacy is easier for both you and your wife?

_____

_____

_____

_____

_____

_____

_____

_____

_____

_____

_____

_____

_____

_____

_____

_____

_____

_____

# A Better Marriage

# You Can Do This

You are here because you want a better marriage. You are here because you want to fix your marriage. You want to be a better husband. You want to have a better wife. You want to have a better home life. You want to like coming home. You want to like coming home to the wife you chose. You want your wife to want to come home to you. You want to a have an affair proof marriage. While that seems impossible, there are things you can do which make it harder for that to happen.

You want a successful relationship and you miss the initial stages of your relationship. You may have even considered divorce, but you really want your marriage because you really love and like your wife. You are still in love with your wife. There are just some relational issues which require your attention.

One of you works longer hours. One of you is too busy to schedule date night. The children take up more time than you imagined. Something is more important than each of you.

What does it take to have a better marriage? What do YOU have to do to have a better marriage? What is your wife complaining about? Have you considered what your wife needs and wants so that you can improve your marriage?

If you do your part totally and completely, then your husband should be influenced to do his part. The law of physics which states for every action, there is an equal and opposite reaction. This same activity exists within relationship. Please respond in love rather than the 'tit for tat' that you are currently using to respond. Most relationships suffer from 'you get me, I get you back.' Please put that down. This is detrimental to the relationship.

Decide to be proactive! What are you going to do to help your relationship? Not what are you going to do if he does something. What are you going to do if he does NOTHING? What are you going to do with YOUR marriage? A Better Marriage comes from within you. You have the availability to change the culture of your relationship.

## The Intensive Retreat for Couples

Remember, for a long time your marriage worked, then something happened and you quit. Maybe it was because she quit or she stopped paying attention to you or you had to compete for her time with the children. Then you stopped washing her car or you stopped being excited when she called. You waited on her to change. She never noticed. Then you got mad. Now you are here.

Do you wish that you handled anything differently? If you could change anything, either action or lack thereof, what would you change? How can you be a better husband? Use the time we have to share how you can be a better husband, what would you plan differently for your marriage, and for yourself.

How important is your marriage to you? Based on that level should give you the desire and motivation to improve your relationship.

Choose a better marriage! Choose a better self! Make a decision to be a game changer in your relationship. Be revolutionary! Take your relationship back!

Love more extravagantly than ever.

Choose forgiveness rather than bitterness and unforgiveness.

Share your heart again.

Use 'tit for tat' in the best possible option. When something great happens, do something greater in response.

Be transparent again—more so than ever.

Remember when you were excited when she called.

Resume that excitement and that excited voice—use it again! And again!

Keep equipping her to successfully respect and love you!

Affirm her ability to be your wife.

Use your love for her to influence her and her heart back to your marriage!

Stop saying things that you will regret!

Stop saying things that you do not mean!

Stop doing things that you will need forgiveness for!

Keep focused on what matters!

Stop keeping quiet when you should be talking!

Remember to start with your best and continue to share your best with your wife!

On a scale of 1 to 10, how would you rate your marriage?

How did you arrive at that number?

Where should your marriage be?

Why do you feel that way?

What are you using to judge that number?

_____

_____

_____

_____

_____

_____

_____

_____

_____

_____

_____

_____

_____

_____

What does it take to get to that ideal number?

Do you need help to get there?

Define help.

_____

_____

_____

_____

_____

_____

_____

_____

_____

_____

_____

_____

_____

_____

_____

_____

_____

_____

Are you willing to work for that place?

What will you have to do to make your marriage better?

What are YOU willing to do to make your marriage whole again?

_____

_____

_____

_____

_____

_____

_____

_____

_____

_____

_____

_____

_____

_____

_____

_____

_____

_____

_____

If God were holding only YOU accountable for this marriage's success, what would He expect YOU to do and to change?

_____

_____

_____

_____

_____

_____

_____

_____

_____

_____

_____

_____

_____

_____

_____

_____

_____

_____

Who are you in this marriage?

Are you your best you?

If not, why not?

When are you going to get to the best you?

Is your lack of you causing your marriage to suffer?

_____

_____

_____

_____

_____

_____

_____

_____

_____

_____

_____

_____

_____

_____

_____

_____

Do you give your best to your wife?

Why not?

What does it take to give your best self to your wife?

Why have you been withholding yourself from your wife?

_____

_____

_____

_____

_____

_____

_____

_____

_____

_____

_____

_____

_____

_____

_____

When did you stop investing in your relationship?

Why did you stop investing in your relationship?

When will you resume investing in your relationship?

_____

_____

_____

_____

_____

_____

_____

_____

_____

_____

_____

_____

_____

_____

_____

_____

_____

What part of your relationship do you miss?

How can you can revive or reintroduce that element back into your relationship?

How did that part of your marriage disappear?

_____

_____

_____

_____

_____

_____

_____

_____

_____

_____

_____

_____

_____

_____

_____

_____

_____

_____

Does your wife think that your marriage needs support?

Why does your wife feel that way?

What does your wife think your relationship needs?

How can that need be achieved?

_____

_____

_____

_____

_____

_____

_____

_____

_____

_____

_____

_____

_____

_____

_____

_____

How can your marriage survive this transition into a great marriage?

_____

_____

_____

_____

_____

_____

_____

_____

_____

_____

_____

_____

_____

_____

_____

_____

_____

_____

**The Intensive Retreat for Couples**

Does the rest of the world, including your children, get the best of you, which means you do not have any energy for your wife, which would include patience and time?

How can you change that circumstance so that you can give your best to your wife?

_____

_____

_____

_____

_____

_____

_____

_____

_____

_____

_____

_____

_____

_____

_____

_____

_____

# Tit for Tat

## And other relationship solutions

## The Final Charge

Did you come because she threatened you with divorce or your best friend just got divorced? Maybe it was because you see a change that you do not like: her indifference. Her attitude made the difference. When she was begging and pleading, you had time to get it right. Now the indifference leaves the house cold, rather than cozy.

You decided that your wife deserved your attention and how you are here.

Men are known for your ability to compartmentalize and zone out at any moment. She does not do that. This marriage is not a checklist item—marriage: check! Marriage is like your biggest client at work. That major portion of your commission check. You take that client to lunch, golf and dinner. You send gifts for major holidays. You call to check in within that decision maker. You know how many kids he has and enough details to keep a meaningful conversation going during that 5 hour round of golf.

Reality check: can you do that with your wife? What is her next major project? What are her plans for the weekend? What did she say in the last conversation? Are you attentive to her? Do you treat her like your best client? If not, why not? What does it take for you to upgrade her to the best level? If you treated her like the client, she would be the priority. She would be first—where she deserves.

What can you do to make her first? She is your wife. You chose her. She accepted you as is. But you do not treat her like she is the best part of your life.

A Better Marriage starts with you. It is about what you do and don't do.

A Better Marriage is a choice. A decision. A set of actions.

# Appendix

Calendar for date nights and special occasions

Marriage Vows

Marriage Goals

Mission, Vision, and Value Statements

Expectations and Heart Rules

Resources

## Calendar for Date Nights

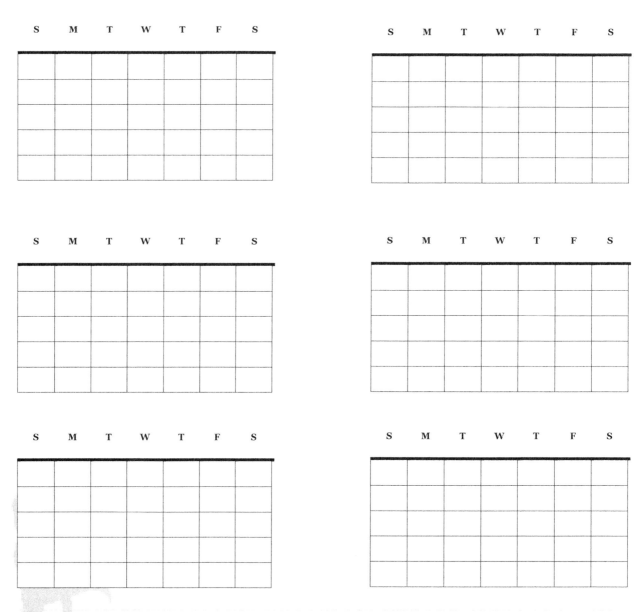

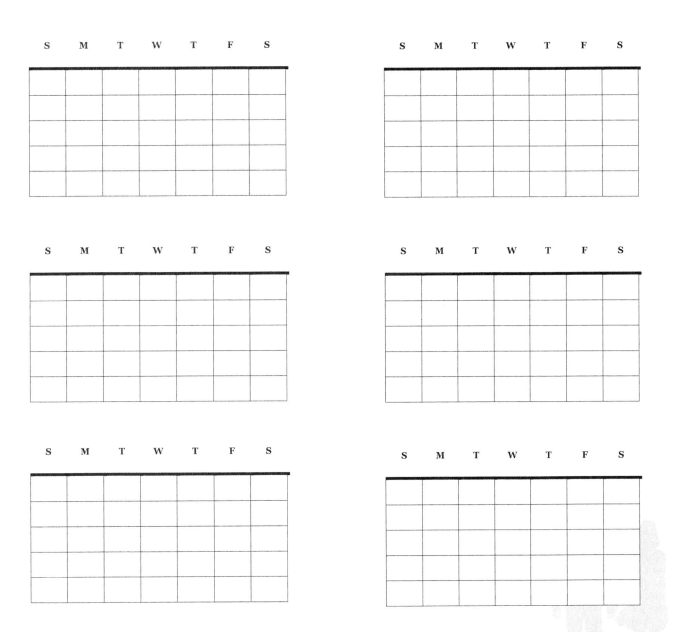

# Marriage Vows

I love you, _____, and I know that God has ordained this love. Because of this I desire to be your husband. Together we will be vessels for His service in accordance with His plan, so that in all areas of our life Christ will have the pre-eminence. Through the pressures of the present and the uncertainties of the future, I promise to be faithful to you. I promise to love, guide, and protect you as Christ does His Church, and as long as we both are alive. According to Ephesians 5 and with His enabling power, I promise to endeavor to show to you the same kind of love as Christ showed the Church when He died for her, and to love you as a part of myself because in His sight we shall be one.

# Marriage Goals

Please establish some goals for your marriage. This is a healthy way to reach a resolve in your marriage. When your needs are met then each spouse feels valued and the marriage will be healthier.

| | | |
|---|---|---|
| How many date nights each month | | |
| Meals together | | |
| Healthy conversations | | |
| Love | | |
| Respect | | |
| Intimacy and Sex (Frequency, etc) | | |
| | | |
| | | |
| | | |
| | | |
| | | |
| | | |
| | | |

# Mission, Vision, and Value

# Statements

Your Mission Statement for your marriage.

_____

_____

_____

_____

_____

_____

_____

_____

_____

_____

_____

_____

_____

_____

_____

Your Vision Statement for your marriage.

_____

_____

_____

_____

_____

_____

_____

_____

Your Values for your marriage.

_____

_____

_____

_____

_____

_____

_____

# Expectations and Heart Rules

**What are your marital expectations? What did you expect from your marriage? Are those expectations being met? If not, have you shared this with your husband?**

_____

_____

_____

_____

_____

_____

_____

_____

_____

_____

_____

_____

_____

_____

_____

_____

_____

_____

**What are your heart rules? (Rules that you live by and what makes your heart happy.)**

_____

_____

_____

_____

_____

_____

_____

_____

_____

_____

_____

_____

_____

_____

_____

_____

_____

_____

_____

# Resources

From Two to One: The Notebook for the Christian Couple by Minister Onedia N. Gage

Getting Away to Get It Together by Bill and Carolyn Wellons

The Love Dare by Alex and Stephen Kendrick

Saving Your Marriage Before It Starts by Drs. Les and Leslie Parrott

Questions Couples Ask by Drs. Les and Leslie Parrott

Powerful Promises for Every Couple by Jim and Elizabeth George

The Christian Husband by Bob Lepine

The Five Love Languages by Gary Chapman

Kingdom Man by Tony Evans

Kingdom Woman by Tony Evans

The Power of a Praying Wife by Stormie Omartian

The Power of a Praying Husband by Stormie Omartian

The Power of Prayer to Change Your Marriage by Stormie Omartian

The Excellent Wife by Martha Peace

The Excellent Husband by Martha Peace

40 Unforgettable Dates with Your Mate by Dr. Gary and Barbara Rosberg

When God Writes Your Love Story by Eric and Leslie Ludy

Love and Respect by Emerson Eggerichs

# ACKNOWLEDGMENTS

God, thank You for Your plans for me. Thank You for *The Intensive Retreat for Couples Her Workbook* and choosing me to complete Your project. I just want to please You. Thank You for continuing to anoint me and to invest in me and my gifts, which keep surprising me. Thank You for loving and forgiving me.

Hillary and Nehemiah, thank you for supporting me and my endeavors. Thank you for loving me, especially when I do nothing without a pen and a clipboard, thank you for enduring my late nights, your ideas, the sounding board, the love and the support. Thank you for celebrating our legacy.

To my prayer partners and to my accountability partners, thank you for the long talks and the powerful prayers and the encouragement.

To the women who this will reach and empower and touch and affect, may these words empower you and help you fervently seek God and reach some resolve. May you be inspired to achieve your goals and dreams. May you enhance your relationship with God so that your other relationships will also improve. May you enhance your self-esteem through prayer and studying. May you have courage and peace. Share love the best you can until you can share love without reservation.

## ABOUT THE HELPER

Minister Onedia N. Gage believes in the study of God's word. She wants women to have the help she wanted and needed as a former wife so that you can grow with your mate. She hopes that you will seek God for a closer relationship so that you can have a closer relationship with your mate.

Take her advice and testimony seriously. Her experience is invaluable. Please use this to reach God. This relationship is ordained by God. Protect it as such.

Minister Onedia invites you to share her study at her retreats for couples. Minister Onedia would like to pray for and with you. Please contact her via email onediagage@onediagage.com

Via twitter @onediangage, on facebook.com/onedia-gage-ministries and phone 512-715-GAGE (4243).

www.youtube.com/onediagage

www.blogtalkradio.com/onediagage

# PREACHER ◆ PRAYER WARRIOR ◆ COACH

To invite Rev. Gage to preach, coach, teach, and pray, Please contact us at

@onediangage (twitter) ◆ onediagage@onediagage.com ◆ facebook.com/onediagage

youtube.com/onediagage ◆ blogtalkradio.com/onediagage ◆ www.onediagage.com

# Publishing

Do you have a book you want to write, but do not know what to do?

Do you have a book you need to publish but do not know how to start?

Would publishing move your career forward?

Let us help

onediagage@purpleink.net ♦ www.purpleink.net

713.705.5530

512.715.4243

CPSIA information can be obtained
at www.ICGtesting.com
Printed in the USA
BVOW08s0054190218
508347BV00021B/250/P